To:

For our grandmothers,
Rose Cooper and Ida Korotkin

Copyright © 1995
Peter Pauper Press, Inc.
202 Mamaroneck Avenue
White Plains, NY 10601
All rights reserved
ISBN 0-88088-620-X
Printed in Hong Kong
7   6   5   4   3   2   1

A GRANDMOTHER IS SOMEONE WHO...

BETH MENDE CONNY

AND

JUDY KOROTKIN

ILLUSTRATED BY

MURRAY CALLAHAN

PETER PAUPER PRESS, INC.
WHITE PLAINS, NEW YORK

Grandmothers are special, no matter how you look at it.

In *A Grandmother is Someone Who . . .* we've looked at it two ways—as a mother turned grandmother (Judy) and as a daughter turned mother (Beth). Our perspectives vary, but we agree on three things:

First, being a grandmother gives you the unique opportunity to step back in time and relive the very best of motherhood, without having to deal with midnight feedings, sibling rivalry, the Terrible Twos or the equally Troublesome Teens.

Second, watching your mother become a grandmother allows you to see yet another side of her and forces you to acknowledge—grudgingly or not—that she *really does* know a thing or two about raising kids.

Third, having a grandmother is one of life's great gifts. Her love, warmth, and wisdom make the world a sweeter place and help you appreciate just how unique you really are.

This collection celebrates the wacky and wonderful world of grandmothers. We hope you will enjoy it and recognize your grandmother, your mother, and yourself within its pages.

J.K. and B.M.C.

A Grandmother is Someone Who . . .

HAS HAIR OF SILVER AND
A HEART OF GOLD.

A Grandmother is Someone Who . . .

LETS YOU WIN AT CARDS.

A Grandmother is Someone Who . . .

MAKES YOU CHICKEN SOUP
EVEN WHEN YOU DON'T
HAVE A COLD.

A Grandmother is Someone Who . . .

HAS RAISED CHILDREN
AND LIVED TO TELL THE TALE.

A Grandmother is Someone Who . . .

LETS YOU HAVE A SECOND
PIECE OF CHOCOLATE

A Grandmother is Someone Who . . .

REMEMBERS EVERYTHING ABOUT
THE GOOD OLD DAYS BUT
CAN'T REMEMBER WHERE SHE
PUT HER GLASSES.

A Grandmother is Someone Who . . .

IS JUST A KID—
ONLY OLDER.

A Grandmother is Someone Who . . .

HAS TURNED FROM ART COLLECTING
TO TOY COLLECTING.

A Grandmother is Someone Who . . .

VOWS TO WAIT 15 MINUTES BEFORE
WHIPPING OUT HER GRANDCHILD'S PHOTO—
AND THEN SETTLES FOR FIVE.

A GRANDMOTHER IS SOMEONE WHO . . .

YOU CAN COME TO WHEN
YOU NEED TO FEEL SMART,
PRETTY, HANDSOME, AND *RIGHT*.

A Grandmother is Someone Who . . .

APPRECIATES THE DIFFICULTIES
OF MOTHERHOOD AND THE
EASE OF GRANDPARENTING.

A Grandmother is Someone Who . . .

BUYS PURSES LARGE ENOUGH
TO HAUL AROUND HER GRANDCHILD'S
PHOTOS, DRAWINGS,
AND REPORT CARDS.

A GRANDMOTHER IS SOMEONE WHO . . .

IS CONVINCED THAT
HER GRANDCHILD RESEMBLES
HER SIDE OF THE FAMILY.

A Grandmother is Someone Who . . .

———— 🐚 ————

ISN'T ASHAMED TO CLUCK LIKE A HEN
OR HOWL LIKE A DOG IF IT MAKES
HER GRANDBABY LAUGH.

A Grandmother is Someone Who . . .

HAS NO PATIENCE FOR THE GAMES
ADULTS PLAY BUT HAS
INFINITE PATIENCE FOR
THE GAMES OF CHILDREN.

A Grandmother is Someone Who . . .

———————— ❧ ————————

SENDS HER CHILD COUNTLESS NEWSPAPER
AND MAGAZINE CLIPPINGS ON
THE IMPORTANCE OF GRANDPARENTS.

A Grandmother is Someone Who . . .

———— ❧ ————

PICKS UP HER GRANDBABY
WHENEVER IT CRIES, EXCEPT FOR
ITS 3 A.M. FEEDING—AN HONOR
RESERVED FOR PARENTS.

A Grandmother is Someone Who . . .

—— ❧ ——

IS ALWAYS WILLING TO LISTEN,
ALTHOUGH SHE CAN'T
ALWAYS HEAR.

A Grandmother is Someone Who . . .

IS THE KEEPER OF
FAMILY MEMORIES, SECRETS,
AND RECIPES.

A Grandmother is Someone Who . . .

————— ❧ —————

HAS A SPECIAL SEAT IN HER HOME
RESERVED FOR LITTLE ONES—
HER LAP.

A Grandmother is Someone Who . . .

ISN'T SHY ABOUT LETTING
YOU KNOW SHE IS THE
FOREMOST AUTHORITY
ON CHILD REARING.

A Grandmother is Someone Who . . .

TREATS YOUR BIRTHDAY AS IF
IT WERE A NATIONAL HOLIDAY.

A Grandmother is Someone Who . . .

HAS REDISCOVERED LOLLIPOPS,
CHOCOLATE KISSES, AND
TUMMY ACHES.

A GRANDMOTHER IS SOMEONE WHO . . .

TELLS YOU THINGS YOU FIND
HARD TO BELIEVE—
LIKE YOUR PARENTS WERE
ONCE KIDS THEMSELVES.

A Grandmother is Someone Who . . .

DENIES SHE CAN'T UNDERSTAND
WHAT HER GRANDBABY IS SAYING
OVER THE TELEPHONE.

A Grandmother is Someone Who . . .

꒷

THINKS RAP IS SOMETHING
YOU WEAR AROUND YOUR SHOULDERS.

A Grandmother is Someone Who . . .

NEVER THINKS YOU'VE
HAD ENOUGH TO EAT.

A Grandmother is Someone Who . . .

———————— ❧ ————————

IS ON A CONSTANT LOOKOUT FOR
THE GAME OR TOY HER
GRANDCHILD *DOESN'T* HAVE.

A Grandmother is Someone Who . . .

— ❧ —

DOESN'T MIND READING HER GRANDSON
THE SAME STORY OVER AGAIN.
AND OVER AGAIN.
AND OVER AGAIN.

A GRANDMOTHER IS SOMEONE WHO . . .

———— 🦢 ————

WON'T LET ANYONE PULL THE WOOL
OVER HER EYES BUT CAN BE
MANIPULATED BY A 3-YEAR-OLD.

A GRANDMOTHER IS SOMEONE WHO . . .

ACTS AS REFEREE BETWEEN
HER CHILDREN AND GRANDCHILDREN.

A GRANDMOTHER IS SOMEONE WHO . . .

IS TEMPTED TO TAKE UP
KNITTING—*AGAIN.*

A Grandmother is Someone Who . . .

PACKS HER CAMERA BEFORE
HER CLOTHES WHEN GETTING
READY FOR A VISIT.

A GRANDMOTHER IS SOMEONE WHO . . .

WANTS TO FIRE THE TEACHER WHO
GAVE HER GRANDSON A "SATISFACTORY"
INSTEAD OF AN "OUTSTANDING"
ON HIS REPORT CARD.

A GRANDMOTHER IS SOMEONE WHO . . .

———————— ❧ ————————

FINALLY HAS AN AUDIENCE
FOR HER FAMILY PHOTO ALBUM.

A GRANDMOTHER IS SOMEONE WHO . . .

IS THE ALL-TIME EXPERT ON
SIBLING RIVALRY AND HAS THE
THERAPIST'S BILLS TO PROVE IT.

A GRANDMOTHER IS SOMEONE WHO . . .

HAS FINALLY FOUND ONE GOOD REASON
FOR GROWING OLDER—GRANDCHILDREN.